MIND RESTORATION & LIFE TRANSFORMATION

The Spiritual and Healing Benefits of Biblical Meditation

DR. COURTNEY DOOKIE

WESTBOW
PRESS®
A DIVISION OF THOMAS NELSON
& ZONDERVAN

WestBow Press books may be ordered through booksellers or by contacting:

WestBow Press
A Division of Thomas Nelson & Zondervan
1663 Liberty Drive
Bloomington, IN 47403
www.westbowpress.com
844-714-3454

Scripture quotations are from the ESV® Bible (The Holy Bible, English Standard Version®), copyright © 2001 by Crossway, a publishing ministry of Good News Publishers. Used by permission. All rights reserved.

ISBN: 978-1-6642-0698-4 (sc)
ISBN: 978-1-6642-0700-4 (hc)
ISBN: 978-1-6642-0699-1 (e)

Library of Congress Control Number: 2020918982

Print information available on the last page.

WestBow Press rev. date: 10/07/2020

Contents

1

Establishing Biblical Meditation

I discovered the miracle of Bible meditation while attending a camp conference in the summer of 2016 with a group of pastors.

The purpose of the camp was to work, play, and worship together, and we sometimes engaged in deep philosophical and theological conversations over lunch or supper. Our conversations were always both uplifting and edifying. At the end of one such conversation, a good friend approached me after everyone had departed and posed a life-changing question. "Courtney," he said with a contemplative pause, "how do we connect to the healing power embedded in the inspired, biblical Word of God?"

I thought about his question for a few minutes then proceeded to answer. But before I share my response, I want to pose the same question to you now: How do *you* connect to the healing power of the inspired Word of God?

Think about it. When you read the sacred Word of God, apart from the explicit commands and instructions, how do you connect with our Father who art in heaven?

The Bible teaches that "anyone in Christ Jesus is a new creation, old things are past, and all things are new" (2 Corinthians 5:17). In other words, there is transformative power rooted in the person of Jesus Christ available to all who follow Him, and it is not dependent on our own behavioral modifications but on God's almighty grace and sovereign power. To be clear, our behaviors change when we follow Jesus, but only by the power of God's Word and the transformative work of the Holy Spirit. But how do we connect with God on a spiritual level?

As you ponder that question, I will share the testimony about my transformation. Though I grew up in Jamaica, which is a more or less Christian culture, I didn't gravitate toward Christianity. I thought all Christians were hypocrites and terrible people who attended church once a week to portray themselves as good people. I had a negative view of God and the church.

I lived my life on my own terms. I figured it was my life, and I didn't need God or anyone else to tell me how to live it. I gambled, engaged in illegal and unethical activities, and led an immoral and dishonest life. On the outside I was quiet, polite, and helpful to most people, but on the inside I was angry and often thought of doing terrible things to people. Only a few close friends knew my dark side.

Without self-control (a fruit of the Holy Spirit), I was quick to violence when people provoked me. On one occasion I threw my best friend into a fence and pressed the point of my knife against his skin when he refused to stop teasing me. On other occasions I did equally disturbing things that hurt my relationships.

Thankfully, my spiritual transformation began during high school when my tenth grade physics teacher—who would have a profound impact on my life—took me under his wing and led me to eventually accepting Jesus Christ as my Lord and Savior.

However, becoming a Christian did not change me overnight. Despite my spiritual progress, my negative thoughts persisted, and at times, I wondered if becoming a Christian was a waste of time. Fortunately, I don't give up on things easily, so I decided to invest more time in getting to know the God of the Bible.

After studying the Bible with commentaries and dictionaries for about six months, I recognized that while I was growing in knowledge and following it to the best of my ability, my understanding was, one might say, mostly legalistic in nature. Hence there was still no genuine change in my mind.

Then one morning I was in my room worshipping when everything changed. While the rain fell outside my window, the proverbial light came shining through when I came across this powerful statement in the book *Mind, Character, and Personality* by E.G. White:

> It would be well for us to spend a thoughtful hour each day in contemplation of the life of Christ. We should take it point by point, and let the imagination grasp each scene, especially the

closing ones. As we thus dwell upon His great sacrifice for us, our confidence in Him will be more constant, our love will be quickened, and we shall be more deeply imbued with His Spirit. If we would be saved, at last, we must learn the lesson of penitence and humiliation at the foot of the cross.

This was my eureka moment, when the lights came on in my mind and the neurons fired in ways they had never fired before. At that moment I realized that in order to be spiritually transformed—for my mind to be changed—I would need to fix my eyes and thoughts on Jesus Christ.

From that day on, I focused on the life of Jesus and other biblical people and immersed myself in biblical stories as if I were there. I spent hours submerged in the various narratives—contemplating, meditating, and praying. Soon, my mind began to change, and negative thought patterns decreased significantly. Not only was I happier and more peaceful inside, but I did better in school and people who knew me observed that there was something different about me.

I share my testimony with you to reinforce this undeniable truth: When the Bible says, "anyone in Christ Jesus is a new creation, old things are past, and all things are new," these are not just words; they are a statement of fact.

Back to the question my friend posed to me at the camp. I answered, "We connect with God when we spend a thoughtful hour in His Word—not just for knowledge but to meditate and immerse ourselves in the narrative. That's when our minds and lives will begin to change in ways that we cannot imagine."

As the apostle Paul said, "Eye has not seen, nor ear heard, nor have entered into the heart of man the things which God has prepared for those who love Him" (1 Corinthians 2:9).

In summary, when we immerse ourselves in the biblical narrative, God harmonizes His Word with our lives. This practice has deepened my belief, faith, and confidence in God's character of love, compassion, care, patience, longsuffering, and trustworthiness. The main goal of Christianity is to experience personal transformation through the Word of God. I will discuss how to access transformation in later chapters, but next I will answer the question, What is biblical meditation?

What is Biblical Meditation?

According to the Holman Illustrated Bible Dictionary, *meditation* is defined as "the act of calling to mind some supposition, pondering upon it, and correlating it to one's own life." The primary biblical reference to meditation is found in the Hebrew scriptures, especially in the book of Psalms.

There are two root words in the Hebrew scriptures for meditation—"hagah" and "siach."

Hagah refers to a gentle cooing involving "frequent reciting of scriptures with a low sounding voice." In the Christian tradition, this is done through singing and the verbal repetition of the Word of God. In the Brown, Driver, and Briggs reference guide, "hagah" is defined as "murmuring in pleasure or anger, to ponder, imagine, talk, mutter, and study" (Brown, Driver, & Briggs, 2008).

Siach means "to be occupied with" or "concerned about" something or someone." This refers to saturating our minds with scriptural principles (such as love, joy, peace, hope, victories through challenges, triumph over tragedy, and lack of faith) until they become part of us.

These same meditation principles are observed in the New Testament scriptures. Brown, Driver, and Briggs define *siach* as "reflection, devotion, beliefs, meditation, musing, study, and prayer" (Brown, Driver, & Briggs, 2008).

Biblical meditation is defined as "a thoughtful focusing of your attention on God's word through Scripture. This includes contemplation of His character of love, morality, and compassion using silence or vocalization to produce positive impacts on [your] thoughts, feelings, and actions" (Brown, Driver, & Briggs, 2008; Dookie, 2017). This sacred practice entails a deep longing to be in the presence of God and thus calls for complete devotion.

The practice is centered on the sacred text of the Bible and includes both the Old and New Testaments. The purpose is to engage and activate the mind, which allows the flow of positive thoughts, actions, and words. In the first chapter of the book of Psalms, the author describes it in terms of engaging the mind, heart, and purpose of life.

To optimize the meditative experience, experts recommend we always do the following things. First, believe God will meet our biopsychosocial-spiritual needs. Second, prepare for each session by reading the biblical Word. This will allow your mind to ponder and grasp the inherent principles within the text/passage (Brown, Driver, and Briggs, 2008).

As is common in all three monotheistic religions, meditation is the act of reflecting on God's past actions in the provision, protection, comfort, and assurance of His love.

Biblical meditation is comparable to many other forms of meditation, but the reality is that the vast majority of biopsychological research is centered on the eastern practice of meditation.

The first commonality of biblical meditation to other meditative exercises is that they all engage in seeking presence. The second commonality is that they all employ a method of dwelling on something or someone (in biblical meditation this focal point is God or the Bible). And the third commonality is seeking—as in the pursuit of a different state. The effects of attention or inattention are all characteristics of meditative practice in general.

In terms of characteristics, biblical meditation can be understood with correlating root words such as "murmur in pleasure or anger, to ponder, imagine, talk, mutter, study, reflect, devotion, beliefs, meditation, contemplation, attention, musing, study, and prayer" (Dookie, 2017).

As Christians, we believe that upon baptism we become one spirit united in Christ (1 Corinthians 12:13; 1 Corinthians 6:17). Therefore, the most critically important goal of biblical meditation is to be in union with Christ. Union with Christ gives the biblical meditation practitioner a true sense of Christ's presence through a moment-by-moment experience with the divine. A prerequisite of biblical meditation is that you believe in the principle of the Bible.

Biblical Meditation and the Brain

Imagine waking in the morning and going into your prayer closet. It is peaceful and quiet. Opening your Bible, you turn to John 8:1-1, which reads:

> "Jesus returned to the Mount of Olives, but early the next morning he was back again at the Temple. A crowd soon gathered, and he sat down and taught them. As he was speaking, the teachers of religious law and the Pharisees brought a woman who had been caught in the act of adultery. They put her in front of the crowd. "Teacher," they said to Jesus, "this woman was caught in adultery. The law of Moses says to

stone her. What do you say?" They were trying to trap him into saying something they could use against him, but Jesus stooped down and wrote in the dust with his finger.

"They kept demanding an answer, so he stood up again and said, "Let the one who has never sinned throw the first stone!" Then he stooped down again and wrote in the dust. When the accusers heard this, they slipped away one by one, beginning with the oldest, until only Jesus was left in the middle of the crowd with the woman. Then Jesus stood up again and said to the woman, "Where are your accusers? Did not even one of them condemn you?"

"No, Lord," she said. Furthermore, Jesus said, "Neither do I. Go and sin no more."

Next, you flip through the pages and land on Luke 8:43-48, which reads:

"Furthermore, a woman having an issue of blood twelve years, who spent all her money on physicians and hadn't been healed, came behind him and touched the border of his garment. Immediately her blood issue stanched. Then Jesus said, 'Who touched me?' When all denied, Peter and the others with him said, 'Master, the multitude throng thee and press thee, and you say, who touched me?'

"Jesus said, 'Somebody touched me, for I perceive that power has gone out of me.' And when the woman saw that she was not hidden, she came trembling and falling before him and declared before all the people how she had touched him and was healed immediately.

"And he said unto her, 'Daughter, be of good comfort: thy faith hath made you whole; go in peace.'

Notice in the first narrative how the woman was caught in the very act of adultery. I know the man was caught too, but for some unfair and unknown reason he was not brought to Jesus. Jesus was fully aware of the woman and her accusers, yet He forgave her sin. Hence, in the most potent way, Jesus upheld the legal penalty for adultery while highlighting the importance of compassion and forgiveness.

In the second account, the woman was rejected and condemned by family, friends, and society just for an illness—an illness that, according to cultural norms, made her unclean and impure. The woman looked beyond her condition, her circumstances, and, most importantly, what others were saying about her, pushed through the crowd, and clung to Jesus. Even though she was unclean, impure, and rejected, she found cleansing, healing, and complete acceptance by clinging to Jesus.

Take some time, transport yourself into one of the above stories. Focus on how He speaks power, purpose, and meaning into these two women's lives. As you do, remember that while we are all guilty of many things, including suffering physical and psychological pains, Jesus always approaches us with love, comfort, tenderness, and compassion.

When we put ourselves into these biblical narratives and imagine that Jesus is speaking the same words of life to us, our brains start to calibrate, our minds start to regulate, and our lives start to emancipate from the pain and suffering we have been enduring.

Biblical meditation increases emotional regulation and impulse control by stimulating brain changes in grey matter within the orbitofrontal cortex. This area of the brain is responsible for emotional regulation, conflict resolution, and decision making. If you are struggling with challenges such as anger, emotional instability, difficulties making current choices, or wanting to do the right thing but doing the wrong thing, biblical meditation can be a great first step to start improving your life.

Back to my story. Before I entered into communion with God, I couldn't see Him through the lens of love. I didn't understand how a loving God allowed me to experience so much pain and suffering. But the moment I started to see God's love through the life of Jesus Christ, greater blood-oxygen signals were supplied to my ventromedial prefrontal cortex (VMPFC).

This prefrontal cortex structure plays a vital role in emotional regulation and inhibiting our response to emotions. I witnessed this in action when the Holy Spirit, through the power of His imperceptible voice, stimulated my ventromedial prefrontal cortex (via my immersion into the life of Jesus Christ through biblical meditation), and empowered me to regulate my anger emotions and my negative response to anger. This change didn't come via my own by behavior modification; it came via the power of God's word. In the pages ahead I will be testifying more about how God has blessed me with conquering power and share how biblical meditation can change your life and give it meaning and purpose.

Think of a teenager or someone who struggles with impulse control. Many people don't know there is a switch in the brain that can help regulate this and many other mental challenges. The switch is called "the middle and superior frontal gyrus." It is known as the "no go" switch because it improves impulse control and risk aversion. Spending time in the presence of God in which we perceive God personally speaking to us can increase grey matter and activity in the superior frontal gyrus and reduce risky behavior.

I think of the dorsolateral prefrontal cortex as the Christian's weapon because it helps us resist temptations. For example, say you are presented with a risky opportunity. An active dorsolateral prefrontal cortex will help override your temptation. Evidence has shown that individuals with an impairment in this brain area tend to fall to temptation easier than those who have no impairments.

There are actually four areas the dorsolateral prefrontal cortex aids: risk-taking, controlling urges, inhibitory functioning, and effective decision making. Persistent and consistent daily biblical meditation will improve the dorsolateral prefrontal cortex's function. and improve your ability to make healthy decisions, evaluate risk more effectively, control impulses, and improve inhibitory functions.

4

Benefits of Biblical Meditation

Build a Trusting Relationship with God

The primary benefit of biblical mediation is that it empowers us to build a deeper and more trusting relationship with God.

Do you sometimes feel like your relationship with God has lost its potency or that the depth of your connection with God is not what it should be? Do you feel like you want more out of your spiritual journey with Jesus? You are not alone; many of us struggle with these same feelings. I know from my personal experience that biblical meditation has the potential to revolutionize your relationship with God.

When building healthy relationships based on trust, friendship is essential. Jesus makes this clear when He says:

"Greater love has no one than this, that someone lay down his life for his friends ... no longer do I call you servants, for the servant does not know what his master is doing. But I have called you friends, for all that I have heard from my Father I have made known to you. (John 15:13-15 ESV).

The Apostle James says in the fulfilled Scripture:

"Abraham believed God, and it was counted to him as righteousness—and he was called a friend of God." (James 2:23 ESV)

These verses emphasize the necessity of friendship with God. Think about your own life. Whom do you trust more: someone you have a deep friendship with or someone you have a causal relationship with?

To build a trusting, friendship-based relationship with God, biblical meditation is highly effective. Biblical meditation allows us to be attuned to God. Attunement facilitates an internal shift in our state of being and enhances resonance, which allows us to enter another person's inner world. In the case of God, we enter the inner world of Jesus Christ. This is what the Apostle Paul was referring to in the following verses when he asked:

> "Who has understood the mind of the Lord to instruct him? Nevertheless, we have the mind of Christ." (1 Corinthians 2:16). And "Have this mind among yourselves, which is yours in Christ Jesus." (Philippians 2:5)

Acquiring the mind of Christ is the essence of attunement and resonance. Resonance is only possible in close relationships because at its core it is the sense of feeling. biblical meditation is a privilege that allows us into the inner chambers of God to experience Him and, in turn, be transformed, empowered, and elevated to a higher, noble purpose.

Another crucial aspect of having a healthy relationship with God is secure attachment. Secure attachment is based on unconditional love. Take a moment and reflect on your relationship with God. How do you see Him? Do you see God as someone who wants to judge you for the wrongs you have done and the wrongs you are doing now? Or do you see Him as a merciful Father who loves you?

The perspective we take of God determines the quality of our relationship with Him. From an attachment theory perspective, "attachment" means "the affectionate bond between an individual and an attachment figure." This bond is evidenced in child and primary attachment figure relationships, such as one between a child and parent. In this type of relationship, the child depends on their parent to fulfill their needs such as: safety, security, shelter, sustenance (food), love, and comfort.

Attachment figures are providers of biological/survival needs, the psychological need for safety, the social need for connection, and—in the context of God—the spiritual need for salvation. To reiterate, there are four basic human needs: survival needs, safety needs, social needs, and the need for salvation. The attachment theory postulates that a child intrinsically, instinctively, and intuitively attaches to a primary attachment figure to fulfill all the aforementioned needs.

Entering into a deep, restorative relationship with God does not come through mere superficial hearing and reading the Bible. If you desire transformation in your spiritual journey, I invite you to meditate on the truth embedded in the Bible. Direct your attention to God's love and mercy, study His excellent grand plan of redemption, allow your mind to be saturated by these themes, and I assure you that your life will change for the better.

Character Formation: Enabling Positive Habits and Reversing Bad Habits

The Bible teaches, "As you think in your heart, so are you." (Proverbs 23:7). Our thought life determines our character.

Think of it like this: thoughts + feelings + habits = character.

I've learned that my character is who I am. Here's a question to ponder: What is your character? Who are you?

Character development starts in our thinking—about ourselves, family, and others. Our thoughts provide us with motivation, direction, and consistency. Our identity as people is essential based on our motives, feelings, and thoughts.

These motives, feelings, and thoughts drive us relationally, emotionally, spiritually, and behaviorally.

Hence, we can conclude that healthy character development is the movement of God's grace towards us in the redemptive activity of Christ. The redemptive work of Christ is to transform our lives. Read this verse and meditate on it:

> "Therefore, if anyone is in Christ, he is a new creation. The old has passed away; behold, the new has come." (2 Corinthians 5:17)

Next, let's take a more in-depth look at what it means to be a new creation in Christ Jesus through the prism of biblical meditation.

Biblical Meditation and Character Transformation

A significant contributing factor to character transformation is a protein called Brain-Derived Neurotrophic Factor (BDNF). It aids the survival of neurons by stimulating their growth, maturation, and maintenance. The BDNF is active between neuron synapses (the gap between two neurons). This is where neuronal communication takes place.

In life, experiences shape us into who we are, good or bad. Each experience causes the synapses to change, adapt, and form new thinking patterns. These thinking patterns release BDNF, which leads to the formation of neural pathways. Neural pathways shape our mindset.

So, how do we change negative mindets to positive mindsets and bad habits to good habits? This is where the power of biblical meditation comes alive! Pick up your Bible and prepare for transformation.

The moment you start monitoring your mind and become aware of your thinking patterns through biblical meditation, your mindset will begin to change. This might seem complicated because we have an estimated seventy-thousand thoughts per day, but nevertheless in time this proactice will empower us to consistently modify our thoughts and thus mindsets.

Monitoring and modifying our thoughts lead to the release of BDNF, which leads to mind transformation. The Bible encourages us to shift our thoughts to heavenly places and things of heavenly nature. In fact, we are instructed to "bring every thought into the captivity of Jesus Christ." (2 Corinthians 10:4)

What does the *captivity of Jesus Christ* mean? It means bringing our thoughts into the fold of His love, grace, peace, and forgiveness.

The ability to modify and adapt the thought process is known as "synaptic plasticity." Brain-Derived Neurotrophic Factor (BDNF) proteins are pivotal to the regulation of synaptic plasticity, which is crucial for memory, encoding, consolidation, and retrieval.

Biblical meditation increases the production of BDNF proteins in the anterior cingulate cortex, lateral ventral cortex, prefrontal cortex, orbitofrontal cortex, and the limbic regions. These brain areas are pivotal for cognitive and emotional function. We can rest easy knowing that God has given our mind the ability to heal itself through the process of neuroplasticity.

Think of BDNF proteins as fertilizers that stimulate growth in brain areas that have been damaged by psychological distress. Biblical meditation activates the production of BDNF and supercharges the fertilization process. Abiding in the presence of God, daily Bible reading of God's promises, and meditating will transform your mind and your life.

The Bible teaches that God loves us with everlasting faithfulness, that we are princes and princesses, and that we are the apples of God's eye. The author E.G. White calls us to walk continually in the light of God:

> "Meditate day and night upon His character. Then you will see His beauty and rejoice in His goodness. Your heart will glow with a sense of His love. You will be uplifted as if borne by everlasting arms. With the power and light that God imparts, you can comprehend more and accomplish more than you ever before deemed possible."

Wow, isn't that powerful? We can have the character of Christ by meditating on the character of Christ. In other words, as our minds abide in Christ, our character is formed into Christ's character.

I invite you to become transformed in character. For heart and mind, this is done by constantly reflecting on Jesus—who loves us so much that he gave Himself for us.

Neutralize the Attacks and Deceptions of the Devil

We live in constant spiritual warfare. This battle is not physical. It is a battle of the mind. This is the most significant form of warfare on the planet. To be victorious in Christ, Paul instructs us in Ephesians 6:10-11:

> "Finally, be strong in the Lord and his mighty power. Put on the full armor of God so that you can take your stand against the devil's schemes."

This verse commands us to prepare for spiritual battle. This is reinforced in 2 Thessalonians 3:3:

> "But the Lord is faithful, and he will strengthen you and protect you from the evil one."

God is faithful. To tap into the faithfulness of God, we must permit Him to enter our minds. In Revelations 3:20, the Apostle John says Jesus stands at our hearts' door and when we let Him into our minds, He takes control and defeats the attacks of the devil on our behalf.

Then, in 2 Corinthians 10:4-5, Paul states:

> "In all these things we are more than conquerors through him who loved us. For I am convinced that neither death nor life, neither angels nor demons, neither the present nor the future, nor any powers, neither height nor depth, nor anything else in all creation, will be able to separate us from the love of God that is in Christ Jesus our Lord."

Are you struggling with addiction, negative thinking, low self-esteem, depression, anxiety, ruminating thoughts? The devil is trying to beat you down. Remember, the Bible says the weapons we fight with are not the weapons of the world. On the contrary, the word of God has divine power to demolish strongholds.

> "We demolish arguments and every pretension that sets itself up against the knowledge of God,

and we take captive every thought to make it obedient to Christ." (2 Corinthians 10:5)

The Apostle Peter encourages us also saying,

"Be alert and of sober mind. Your enemy, the devil, prowls around like a roaring lion looking for someone to devour. Resist him, standing firm in the faith, because you know that the family of believers throughout the world is undergoing the same suffering." (1 Peter 5:8)

Being alert and sober-minded means to direct our minds to the presence of God. When we do this, we activate the following brain areas: cortical, which includes the frontal (executive functions), temporal (aid in the formation of long-term memory and regulate emotion), and parietal lobes (integrate sensory information); the subcortical or limbic system, which consists of the amygdala (emotional learning, emotional detection, and reward system) thalamus (relay station of the brain), hippocampus (important for memory), hypothalamus (regulate body temperature, controlling of appetite, managing of sexual behavior, regulating emotional responses), and basal ganglia (important for motivation, decision making, and working memory) ; and the brain stem (regulate automatic functions of the body), which includes the reticular formation, pons, medulla, locus coeruleus, nucleus raphe, and sensory triennium nucleus.

The activation of these brain areas empowers us to resist the attack of the devil. Meditating on God's word will give you the power to resist the devil; under the power of Christ he will flee.

In fighting this spiritual battle, we first must ask God to give us the strength to defeat what is called "busyness," which is one of the primary ways the devil attacks God's children. When we are too busy, we tend to read the Bible very hastily or not at all. Know this: a hasty reading of the Scriptures will not empower you to defeat the enemy. The Psalmist writes:

"Thy word have I hid in my heart that I might not sin against you." (Psalm 119:11)

My friend keep the Bible with you. When an opportunity presents itself, read it. Etch the texts in your memory. When you go about reading a passage, meditate on it and fix it in mind. This is how you can and will neutralize the attacks and deceptions of the devil.

Enhance Peace of Mind: Reduces Stress, Worry, Fear, and Anxiety

We live in a world today that is imprisoned by fear and anxiety. Fear is used by pastors, politicians, parents, and prelates to force others into subjection. The year 2020 alone has seen one of history's worst fears: the fear of novel Coronavirus—Covid-19. All around us, we see fear and anxiety bringing people to their knees and imprisoning their minds. I'm here to tell you practicing daily biblical meditation reduces the impact of fear and anxiety.

Fear has a tremendous negative impact on our health. It weakens the immune system, promotes cardiovascular and gastrointestinal problems, decreases fertility, speeds up the aging process, and leads to premature death. Fear also disrupts brain activities and impairs long-term memory. The hippocampus is the brain structure responsible for long-term memory encoding, when this brain area is impaired, it is difficult to regulate fear and anxiety follows. If those things aren't enough, fear also degrades our ability to regulate emotions and make critical decisions and increases reactivity and impulsivity.

From a neurobiological perspective, fear and anxiety affect the three fundamental brain regions: the brain stem, the limbic system, and the cortical area. Weakness in these regions disrupts cognitive ability, emotional regulation, and the sleep-wake cycle. Fear, stress, and anxiety activates the hypothalamic-pituitary-adrenal axis leading to the release of stress hormone. The consistent release of stress hormones can lead to multiple sicknesses and diseases.

The Bible tells us not to give room to unhealthy fear. It tells us, "God has not given us a spirit of fear, but of love, power, and a sound mind (2 Timothy 1:7). Notice what God has given to us: love, power, and a sound mind.

The Bible also declares, "Perfect love casts out fear." (1 John 4:18). I want to expand on that further: perfect love casts out fear *and* rebuilds brain pathways. Who or what is the "perfect love"? It is Jesus Christ.

Biblical meditation increases grey matter in the brainstem. This means that contemplation on the love of Christ activates changes in the brainstem, which positively impacts the brainstem's function and structure. The limbic system or emotional brain receives positive stimulation from biblical meditation. Imagine that: thinking about God's love can change the structure and function of your brain through neuroplasticity. *Wow!*

Biblical meditation initiates neuroplasticity in the limbic system. This improves emotional regulation, aids in the recovery from anxiety, depression, post-traumatic stress disorder, developmental trauma disorder, borderline personality disorder, disruptive mood dysregulation disorder, anger, irritability, and suicidality. Meditation and prayer increase activity and grey matter in the frontal lobe, dorsolateral prefrontal cortex, ventromedial prefrontal cortex, and the anterior cingulate cortex.

Furthermore, biblical meditation facilitates brain changes in the frontal lobe, dorsolateral prefrontal cortex, ventromedial prefrontal cortex, and the anterior cingulate cortex. Reciting and meditating on biblical text increases the activity in the frontal-parietal circuit.

Science supports every word of the Bible. Recent findings report that ventral medial prefrontal cortex (VMPFC), dorsolateral prefrontal cortex (DLPFC), hippocampus, parahippocampal gyrus, middle temporal gyrus, temporal pole, and retrosplenial cortex are more active in individuals who practice daily meditation.

Meditation triggers the brain's ability to initiate neurogenesis and activates neuroplasticity in all of the above brain areas. This gives individuals who have challenges with fear and anxiety or mental disorders the opportunity to receive the healing God intended. Imagine this: just spending *time* with God can reduce anxiety, fear, and stress and give to peace of mind!

Take note of Christ's words:

> "My peace I leave you, my peace I give you. I do
> not give to you as the world gives. Do not let
> your heart be troubled and do not be afraid. I

have said these things to you, that in me you may have peace ..." (John 14:27)

The Prophet Isaiah says:

"And the effect of righteousness will be peace, and the results of righteousness, quietness, and trust forever." (Isaiah 32:17)

Paul says:

"Therefore, since we have been justified by faith, we have peace with God through our Lord Jesus Christ." (Romans 5:1)

There are numerous other verses that talk about the peace that God desires to lavish us with. Are you open to receive His peace and receive healing for worry, guilt, and fear?

Fortify Your Mind to Receive Forgiveness and Give Forgiveness

Jane was sexually, physically and emotionally abused by someone who her family considered to be a family friend. Later in life her abuser became a Christian and sort to apologized to Jane for what he had done to her.

Jane said, "I cannot forgive, the pain is too much." Have you ever been there or are you there now? Where someone did something to you that hurts so deep that you cannot see how it is possible to forgive them?

In life, everyone goes through hurtful events caused by significant others, a deceptive friend, a betraying partner, or an unjust parent who falsely accuses. In response to painful emotions, we often react with anger, hostility, and the desire for revenge. As an alternative, we can decide to forgive the wrongdoer and relinquish resentment.

Forgiveness is a difficult decision because we often mistakenly believe if we forgive the one who caused us pain, we will be letting them go free. The reality is, forgiveness liberates *us* from the pain they caused. Forgiveness happens when someone who has been wronged chooses to let go of their resentment and treat themselves and the wrongdoer with kindness and compassion.

Like fear, unforgiveness has a negative effect on psychological, physiological, spiritual, and relational health.

Some of the adverse effects of unforgiveness include disruption of healthy cardiovascular activity, impoverishment, sleep deprivation, production of stress hormones, depression, chronic emotional distress, fear, and anxiety.

Listen to what Jesus said:

> "If you are offering your gift at the altar and remember that your brother or sister has something against you, leave your gift there before the altar and go. First, be reconciled to your brother, and then come and offer your gift." (Matthew 5:23-24).

Notice in this verse that if someone has something against you, even if you don't have something against them, you should be willing to connect with them and seek to reconcile. Forgiveness is a choice; the one who experiences offense must choose to forgive.

Keep in mind, just because you choose to forgive does not mean the other person will (or must) reciprocate. Forgiveness is not about the other person; it is to free you from the pain of the wound. After all, sometimes offenses committed against us are so disturbing that it is impossible to be in the offender's physical presence. In that case, I recommend you spend time alone in God's presence, reflecting on your willingness to set the offender free and free yourself from the pain.

In contrast to unforgiveness, biblical meditation on the principle of forgiveness is linked with positive emotional states. Forgiveness activates the brain network and leads to empathy and regulation of emotion through cognition. In fact, the willingness to forgive someone has a positive impact on the precuneus, right inferior parietal regions, dorsolateral prefrontal cortex, medial prefrontal cortex, cingulate gyrus, and the ventral medial prefrontal cortex.

Biblical meditation activates the above brain areas, thus aiding in emotional regulation, resolving anger and resentment, improving interpersonal relationships, improving self-esteem, and reducing heart rate. Research indicates that forgiveness represents a positive, "healthy" strategy for us to overcome challenges that otherwise would lead to significant psychological and neurobiological stress.

Take some time to meditate on the Lord's prayer in Matthew 6 and give specific attention to verse 6:

The Lord's Prayer

"Our Father in heaven, who art in heaven, hallowed be your name. Your kingdom come, your will be done, on earth as it is in heaven. Give us this day, our daily bread, and forgive us our debts, as we also forgive our debtors. Moreover, lead us not into temptation but deliver us from evil. Amen."

Allow this prayer to permeate your mind and sink into your heart: "Forgive us our debts, as we also forgive our debtors." This will create a catalyst for transformation in your brain and lead to healing and restoration.

Increase Emotional Intelligence

The biblical definition of emotional intelligence is embedded in the following verse, " ...the second commandment is this: 'Love your neighbor as yourself ...'"

By definition, emotional intelligence is our ability to recognize our emotional state and the emotional states of those in our environment. Emotional intelligence also entails regulating emotions effectively in ourselves and our relationships. In other words, we must be open to monitor and modify our minds. This capability allows us to be versatile and adjust our emotions to the requirements of the present moment.

There are four categories of emotional intelligence: spiritual, physical, psychological, and relational.

Spiritual Emotional Intelligence

Emotion comes from the Latin word, "motrre," which means "to move," plus the prefix "e," which means to "move away." This definition indicates emotions urge us to *do* something. Spiritual emotional intelligence has three components: our connection to God (Divine Connection), our connection to our spiritual state (Personal Connection), and our connection to what God is doing in and through us (Redemptive Connection). To boost spiritual emotional intelligence, we should seek Bible passages that talk about each of the above components. Below I have provided an example for each.

Divine Connection. "I am the vine; you are the branches. If you remain in me and I in you, you will bear much fruit; apart from me, you can do nothing. If you do not remain in me, you are like a branch thrown away that withers; such branches are picked up, thrown into the fire and burned. If you remain in me and my words remain in you, ask whatever you wish, and it will be done for you. (John 15:5)

Personal Connection. "Search me, O God, and know my heart; Try me and know my anxious thoughts." (Psalm 139:23)

Redemptive Connection. "From now on, therefore, we regard no one according to the flesh. Even though we once regarded Christ according to the flesh, we regard him thus no longer. Therefore, if anyone is in Christ, he is a new creation. The old has passed away; behold, the new has come. All this is from God, who through Christ reconciled us to Him and gave us the ministry of reconciliation. In Christ, God was reconciling the world to Him, not counting their trespasses against them, and entrusting to us the message of reconciliation. Therefore, we are ambassadors for Christ, God making his appeal through us. We implore you on behalf of Christ be reconciled to God. For our sake he made him be sin who knew no sin so that in him we might become the righteousness of God." (2 Corinthians 5:16-21)

Physical Emotional Intelligence

Emotional intelligence is linked to improved physical health. Numerous researchers have indicated that emotional intelligence boosts protective factors against heart disease, better management of type 2 diabetes, chronic pain, some type of cancers, obesity, headaches, gastrointestinal problems, and premature death. The mind controls all aspects of what it means to be human. Every action, good or bad, have their source in the mind. Our health and development are hinged on the harmonious action of all systems of our bodies. All the physical organs are the servants of the mind, and the nerves are the messengers that transmit its orders to every part of the body, guiding the motions of the living machinery. The electric power that biblical meditation supplies to the brain promotes mental activity, vitalizes the whole system, and is thus an invaluable aid in resisting sickness and diseases.

I invite you today to develop a Christo-centric meditative practice in order to tap into the power that the mind has over the body. The practice of biblical meditation will facilitate circulation oxygenated blood throughout the central nervous system. Thus, aid in both prevention and healing of the body from sickness.

Psychological Emotional Intelligence

Emotional intelligence enhances psychological well-being. Mental health challenges affect one in four people in North America. Hence, those with lower emotional intelligence may suffer more from depression, anxiety, substance use, addiction, and personality disorders. Emotional intelligence empowers us to regulate impulse control and emotions, as well as manage external pressures and stress, including the facets of emotion regulation, stress management, and impulsiveness. Biblical mediation empowers us to have a contented mind, and a cheerful spirit. Having a contented mind and a cheerful spirit will increase our ability to manage the symptoms associated with mental disorders.

Relational Emotional Intelligence

Do you realized that we are all woven together in the great web of humanity, and whatever we can do to benefit, and uplift others will reflect in blessing upon ourselves? The law of mutual dependence runs through all classes of society. (EG White, 1890).

Emotional intelligence fosters our ability to identify and express feelings and maintain close relationships with significant others. This includes aspects of emotion perception, emotion expression, empathy, and relationships. It also increases our ability to assert ourselves in interpersonal relationships and helps us with the tools to influence others ' emotions and decisions effectively.

Now let's consider emotional intelligence in the context of biblical meditation. Emotional intelligence positively affects the following brain areas, anterior insula (AI), amygdala, orbitofrontal cortex (OFC), anterior cingulate cortex (ACC), and ventromedial prefrontal cortex (vmPFC). The AI is essential for empathy. It is activated in response to other people's pain, and to expressions of disgust, fear and happiness.

Biblical meditation activates the anterior insula, when the AI is activated it enhances my ability to have empathy. Empathy is my ability to perceive, understand and experience others' feelings in relation to ones' self.

The anterior insula and anterior cingulate cortex are vital for producing emotional awareness and the ability to perceive feelings of oneself, while the amygdala and ventromedial prefrontal cortex are essential for understanding the emotional state of those in our environment. Helping to assess and regulate our emotions, the orbitofrontal cortex mediates our ability to adjust emotional expression by reasonably evaluating the salient emotional stimuli and regulating our subjective emotional experience.

It is fascinating to know and understand that biblical meditation positively impacts all the aforementioned brain areas. Thus, biblical meditation enhances our aptitude to develop healthy emotional intelligence.

Meditative Biblical Techniques

After learning the art and science of biblical meditation and benefitting from it greatly, I turned my attention to teaching others through seminars.

In my seminars, people often ask me to share specific biblical meditation methods. In this chapter I will share six techniques I recommend. These six techniques are also used in other forms of meditation.

Biblical meditation is centered on God's love towards us and our love towards ourselves and others. This kind of meditation includes loving-kindness and compassion; visualization of love; focusing attention on God/awareness; openly monitoring our hearts; praying for self, others and the universe; breathing in the love; experiencing peace and joy; awareness of God's faithfulness; and relaxation. I will discuss these elements of biblical meditation in the context of neuroplasticity and psychological pain healing in later chapters.

Biblical Focused Attention Meditation

Biblical focused attention meditation is exactly what it sounds like: we choose a text, a passage, or theme in the Bible and then invest our full attention on it for a set amount of time. To begin this practice, I recommend starting with six to eight minutes sessions with the goal of building your way to about an hour daily. The more you practice, the more you will become comfortable. There are six steps to biblical focused attention meditation.

Step one is to find a quiet and comfortable place either in your home or outside. We need a place where we can distinguish the still, small voice of God amid all the noise around us.

Step two is to find a comfortable position. This may include sitting, kneeling, laying down, or standing. The key is to be comfortable. Be aware that you do not want to be so comfortable you fall asleep.

Step three is to choose the time of day that works best for you. Choose the time that is best for you. Some people choose morning and evening, midday and evening, or morning and midday—it does not matter. Just choose the time that is most comfortable for you.

Step four is to choose a text, passage, or theme from the Bible to focus your attention. To illustrate this step, let us use one of the passages we used in chapter two: the woman with the hemorrhaging problem. Now that you have selected a passage, we can move to step five.

Step five is to fix your attention on the theme, text, or passage you have chosen. Bring your complete attention to the scene described by the text. The woman has been suffering for twelve years—rejected and cast out for being impure and unclean. Her family, friends, place of worship, and society treat her with disdain and scorn.

Take a trip into her mind and try to feel her physical pain and psychological agony. Next, shift your attention to another part of her mind in which she sees hope because of what she heard Jesus was doing for others who were sick. Notice how hope energizes her to push through her mental agony, the crowd, and others' voices.

Now move your attention to her movements toward Jesus. She is convinced by faith that He has the power to heal her malady. Look at her as she touches Jesus and witness His healing power flowing into her body. See Jesus turning his attention to her and how she receives physical healing. Think about how Jesus is going to restore her to a rightful place in society and the place of worship.

Hear the voice of Jesus saying to her, "Be of excellent comfort, your faith has made you well; go in peace."

Transport yourself into the narrative and believe that with the power of Jesus you can conquer any challenge you are dealing with in life. Maybe you have been dealing with psychological, physiological, relational, or spiritual challenges for years and nothing has helped you overcome it. Picture yourself with the same healing faith as the woman in the narrative and *believe* in the healing power of Jesus to restore you.

Step six is to notice when distracting thoughts enter your mind and then gently shift your attention back to your chosen text. The emphasis of this type of meditation is God and His actions in the life of humanity. As you let go and release your fears and anxieties, direct your mind to Jesus and His teachings by reading the scriptures and permitting your mind to be saturated with it. Focus on how the events in the scriptures can be applied to your daily life.

Biblical Open Monitoring Meditation

In Open Monitoring Meditation, we become aware of our thoughts and emotions without judgment.

As we encounter Bible themes, we experience various emotions and thoughts. With the Open Monitoring technique, the idea is to resist the temptation to change our thoughts or feelings. The goal is to simply observe our thoughts from a non-judgmental perspective.

Similar to biblical-focused attention meditation, Open Monitoring reduces activity in the brain's "default mode network," which is responsible for mind wandering. This daily practice has the potential to infuse you with the ability to direct and maintain conscious attention in the present moment and reduce mind wandering. "Mindfulness," as it is called, is considered a crucial skill needed to overcome anxiety disorders.

In summary, Open Monitoring biblical meditation entails non-reactive and non-judgment awareness of our thoughts while being conscious of the present moment and improves our well-being, happiness, memory, and concentration. This is how you can experience your bodily sensations, feelings, and thoughts.

People often ask me: "What are the components of open monitoring biblical meditation?"

To effectively practice this meditation, I recommend setting set aside ten to fifteen minutes every day in a quiet place. Once you are settled in a comfortable position, read a Bible narrative—for example, Jesus' journey from Gethsemane to the cross. Then close your eyes to avoid visual distractions, focus on your breath and feel your lungs expand and contract.

Notice the sensations along the surface of your skin as well as any sounds or movement in your environment. Shift your awareness to your internal working; that is, what is happening in your body, mind, and Spirit. Remember to simply witness it without reacting or judging the experience. If your mind wanders, shift your awareness back to the place of monitoring.

Let us try this using the example of Jesus' journey from Gethsemane to the cross.

The Journey of Jesus Through the Practice of Open Monitoring Meditation

Let us take a journey to the brook of Kidron. It is located between Jerusalem and the Mount of Olives in a garden called Gethsemane. As Jesus and His disciples enter the garden, notice the Bible says, "Judas, the one who betrayed Him, also knew the place."

Let's consider the various stages of this narrative. In stage one, shortly after Jesus entered the garden, Judas, the troops, and officers from the chief priest and Pharisees came to arrest Jesus. In stage two, Jesus is bound and dragged away to Annas to be judged. In stage three, Peter, one of Jesus's disciples, declares that he does not know Jesus. In stage four, a thief is chosen over Jesus. In stage five, soldiers mock and beat Jesus. In stage six, Pilate sentenced Jesus to death. In stage seven, the soldiers gambled for Jesus' garment. In stage eight,

Jesus's mother, friends, and disciples painfully witnessed His suffering on the cross: the nails in His hands, the thorns on His head, His side pierced, and finally His death.

As you have probably observed, it is easy to get distracted by feelings, sensations, and thoughts when we read about this deeply disturbing event and Christ's suffering. In fact, Peter is so distracted by his feelings that he attacks one of the soldiers. That is, the essential purpose of Jesus' mission on earth was about start, but Peter was distracted by his feelings, sensations, and thoughts.

Imagine being there and witnessing the events at each stage starting in the garden. Become aware of your experience. Notice the sensation on the surface of your skin. Feel the air in the garden. Imagine the sounds and movement all around you. Sense your awareness glowing in all directions. Mentally scan the garden and simply witness the moment as it is. If your mind wanders, shift your awareness back to your experience in the garden without reacting or judging.

Notice your feelings, sensations, and thoughts towards Judas, Peter, Pilate, the priests, the soldiers, Jesus's disciples, His mother, and other friends. Be present in the experience and try not to be distracted by your feelings, sensations, and thoughts. This practice will reduce activity in your anterior medial prefrontal cortex and posterior cingulate cortex, which are vital to the default mode network.

During this time, we should openly monitor our connection with the narrative. When I read it, I feel guilt and shame when I am reminded of what I have done to contribute to the sufferings of Christ. These two emotions have the potential to deregulate and disrupt my neurological integration. If I allow the feelings, sensations, and thoughts to distract me, I could miss the essential work of salvation that God is doing in my life.

To be sure, in my desperation to change, I must avoid judging and reacting, or I might prematurely transition to the conclusion of Christ's passion on the cross without experiencing His journey from Gethsemane. Hence, I must be open to monitor myself and allow all the pain, suffering, guilt, and shame to pass from Gethsemane to the cross.

When we monitor without reacting or judging, we can see how Jesus delivers us from our shame, guilt, and suffering without our active participation. In that case, the journey becomes a passive experience in which the work, word, and wonderous power of Jesus can transform my life. It brings me to awareness and understanding that He has paid the price, and in turn I can accept His gift of well-being and restoration. Alas, I am liberated from feeling anxious or fearful and can truly embrace well-being, integration, happiness, and improved memory and concentration.

Biblical Mindfulness Meditation

In the practice of biblical mindfulness, our goal is to develop an awareness of the present moment's experience through a perceptible mental process. This practice seeks to engage the mind to pay attention and focus on becoming aware of the present moment with intention and purpose. Specifically, we aim to become aware of the self in the present moment and how God is interacting with us at that moment.

Unlike biblical open monitoring meditation, with biblical Mindfulness meditation we seek to become aware of our purpose and intention.

You might realize by now that the various meditative practices have some overlap, but they are different when it comes to how each interacts with the mind. Notice the two keywords in biblical mindfulness: "intention" and "purpose." Think of it this way, when we enter the presence of God, we intend to change and to understand our purpose in life. Through this process we experience intentional change.

Read the following twenty original verses in the Bible. Each of them includes the word *meditation*. As you read, look out for intention and purpose. Also, consider how the intentions and purposes in these verses apply to your life.

1. Genesis 24:63. "And Isaac went out to meditate in the field toward evening. Furthermore, he lifted his eyes and saw and behold; camels were coming."

2. Joshua 1:8. "This Book of the Law shall not depart from your mouth, but you shall meditate on it day and night, so that you may be careful to do according to all that is written in it. For then, you will make your way prosperous, and then you will have success."

3. Psalm 1:2. "But his delight is in the law of the Lord, and on his law, he meditates day and night."

4. Psalm 5:1. "Give ear to my words, O Lord, Consider my meditation."

5. Psalm 19:14. "Let the words of my mouth and the meditation of my heart be acceptable in your sight, O Lord, my rock, and my redeemer."

6. Psalm 49:3. "My mouth shall speak wisdom; the meditation of my heart shall be understanding."

7. Psalm 63:6. "When I remember you upon my bed and meditate on you in the watches of the night ..."

8. Psalm 77:12. "I will ponder all your work and meditate on your mighty deeds."

9. Psalm 104:34. "May my meditation be pleasing to him, for I rejoice in the Lord."

10. Psalm 119:15. "I will meditate on your precepts and fix my eyes on your ways."

11. Psalm 119:23. "Even though princes sit plotting against me, your servant will meditate on your statutes."

12. Psalm 119:48. "I will lift my hands toward your commandments, which I love, and I will meditate on your statutes."

13. Psalm 119:78. "Let the insolent be put to shame because they have wronged me with falsehood; as for me, I will meditate on your precepts."

14. Psalm 119:97. "Oh how I love your law! It is my meditation all day."

15. Psalm 119:99. "I have more understanding than all my teachers, for your testimonies are my meditation."

16. Psalm 119:148. "My eyes are awoken before the watches of the night, that I may meditate on your promise."

17. Psalm 143:5. "I remember the days of old; I meditate on all that you have done; I ponder the work of your hands."

18. Isaiah 33:18. "Your heart will meditate on terror: Where *is* the scribe? Where *is* he who weighs? Where *is* he who counts the towers?"

19. Luke 21:14. "Settle it therefore in your minds not to meditate beforehand how to answer."

20. 1 Timothy 4:15. "Meditate on these things; give yourself entirely to them, that your progress may be evident to all."

The key themes of biblical mindfulness are based on the law of Love, the word of Love, the works of Love, and the way of Love. Jesus, in responding to the religious leaders of His time about the divine constitution of the law, said:

> "You shall love the Lord your God with all your heart, with all your soul, and with all your mind. This is *the* first and greatest commandment. And *the* second *is* like it: You shall love your neighbor as yourself." (Matthew 22:34-39)

The central focus of the Law is love; the Bible tells us *God is Love.*

Follow the same steps from above for focused biblical meditation. Notice step four is a bit more involved this time.

Step one is to find a quiet and comfortable place either in your home or outside. We need a place where we can distinguish the still, small voice of God amid all the noise around us.

Step two is to find a comfortable position. This may include sitting, kneeling, laying down, or standing. The key is to be comfortable. Be aware that you do not want to be so comfortable you fall asleep.

Step three is to choose the time of day that works best for you. Choose the time that is best for you. Some people choose morning and evening, midday and evening, or morning and midday—it does not matter. Just choose the time that is most comfortable for you.

Step four is to choose a text, passage, or theme from the Bible to focus your attention. This is called biblical mindfulness. Here, we are allowing the mind to be saturated with the primary theme of the Bible, that is, Jesus Christ.

To begin this practice, I recommend starting with 15 minutes in the morning and focusing on whatever subject you have chosen until noon. At noon, take 15 minutes to review the same theme a second time, then continue to be mindful of the theme until the day ends. 15 minutes before bedtime, review the same theme and seek to understand how it correlated with the events of your day and helped you. And don't forget to give God thanks. Here's a "cheat sheet" to help you.

- *15 minutes in the morning.* Select a theme in the morning for worship. Keep the theme active in mind.

- *15 minutes at noon.* Review and refresh the theme in the context of the day's events. Ask yourself: "What are my thoughts, emotions, and sensations? What events have changed them since the morning? Maintain the theme in the mind.

- *15 minutes before bedtime.* Review the same theme in the evening for worship before bed. Reflect and see how the theme contributed to your productivity throughout the day.

As a practitioner of this type of meditation, I have experienced a greater sense of peace and calmness throughout my day. For instance, if I become too busy and do not initiate my mindfulness practice in the morning, I find I am less effective in managing challenges I encounter.

The enemy of the mind wants to distract us with busyness, so we neglect the most vital aspect of our lives. Be aware that there is no higher, important work you and I can engage in than training our minds. When we train our minds by mindfully meditating on God's word, God empowers us to nurture His purpose for our lives.

Ask yourself this question: When I go to God, is it my intention that He transform my mind so I can have a deeper understanding of my purpose?

"Do not conform to the pattern of this world but be transformed by the renewing of your mind." (Romans 12:2)

Knowing and understanding the enemy of the mind is continually trying to deregulate the mind's integration is of extreme importance. God has given us the Bible and His Spirit so that He can transform our minds. By structuring your mind through the prism of a deliberate forty-five minute per day meditation session, you can elevate your life to live your full purpose.

With biblical mindfulness, we become mindful of Christ's teachings, Christ's sympathies, Christ's grace, and Christ's peace. This enables us to be empowered in moments of disempowerment. Christ sees in us infinite possibilities; therefore, He encourages us to come unto Him to find rest and peace so we can realize those infinite possibilities.

The question is, do you want to combat the enemy's power over your mind? If your answer is yes, then ask God for the power to invest forty-five minutes per day in meditative practice. Rest assured your efforts will transform your mind, your life, and the lives of those in your environment.

Biblical Loving-Kindness Meditation

In biblical loving-kindness meditation, we incorporate principles from both focus attention, open monitoring, and mindfulness meditation. The practitioner focuses on Jesus Christ (the object) and the work of love and compassion that He demonstrated towards humanity. In loving-kindness meditation, the meditator develops Christ's love and compassion for him or herself, extending that love and compassion towards others.

Biblical loving-kindness meditation stimulates positive feelings of warmth, happiness, and joy in a person. It begins by developing a loving feeling toward God and self, and then extending those feelings towards families, friends, acquaintances, colleagues, and all humanity. It is like Jesus says:

"Love the Lord your God with all your heart, and with all your soul, and with all your mind, and with all your strength. The second commandment is this: love your neighbor as yourself. There is no commandment greater than these." (Mark 12:30-31)

Two fundamental principles are embedded in biblical loving-kindness meditation.

Principle Number One: Self-Care

Self-love is care for yourself (self-care). We live in a society that forces us to comply with unrealistic demands, especially to keep up with the Joneses. In our pursuit of these demands, we create stress and tension in our bodies.

STOP HERE.

Is the pace of your life going fast? Do you feel like you are being driven by many forces that appear to be beyond your control? When was the last time you took some time to take care of yourself?

If you cannot answer the last question and your answer to the previous question is yes, then it is time for you to stop and take back your life. Stress and tension lead to depression, anxiety, substance use, broken families, inflexibility, and hopelessness.

Are you one of those individuals who think you are not worthy or deserving? I am inviting you to decide today to engage deeply in loving-kindness meditation.

In loving-kindness meditation, we seek to create feelings of kindness and warmth towards ourselves and others. To start this practice, commit yourself to 30 minutes of meditation per day. Here are the main steps:

The first step is to find a quiet and comfortable place either in your home or outside. We need a place where we can distinguish the still small voice of God amid all the noise around us.

Step two is to find a comfortable position. This may include sitting, kneeling, laying down, or standing. The key is to be comfortable. Remember, you do not want to be so comfortable you fall asleep.

Step three is to choose the best time of day that works for you. Some people choose morning and evening, midday and evening, or morning and midday—it does not matter. Just chose what you are most comfortable with.

Step four is to choose from the following verses. All the verses below are taken from the ESV.

- 1 Corinthians 6:19. "Or do you not know that your body is a temple of the Holy Spirit within you, whom you have from God? You are not your own ..."

- 1 John 3:1. "See what kind of love the Father has given to us, that we should be called children of God; and so, we are. The reason why the world does not know us is that it did not know him."

- Romans 5:8. "But God shows his love for us in that while we were still sinners, Christ died for us."

- John 3:16. "For God so loved the world, that he gave his only Son, that whoever believes in him should not perish but have eternal life."

- 1 John 4:14. "So we have come to know and to believe the love that God has for us. God is love, and whoever abides in love abides in God, and God abides in him."

- John 15:9-17. "As the Father has loved me, so have I loved you. Abide in my love. If you keep my commandments, you will abide in my love, just as I have kept my Father's commandments and abide in his love. These things I have spoken to you, that my joy may be in you, and that your joy may be full. This is my commandment that you love one another as I have loved you. Greater love has no one than this: that someone lay down his life for his friends."

- John 15:13. "Greater love has no one than this: that someone lay down his life for his friends."

- 1 John 3:1. "See what kind of love the Father has given to us, that we should be called children of God; and so, we are. The reason why the world does not know us is that it did not know him."

- Galatians 2:20. "I have been crucified with Christ. It is no longer I who live, but Christ who lives in me. And the life I now live in the flesh I live by faith in the Son of God, who loved me and gave himself for me."

The first verse tells us that we are the temple of God. In other words, it is in us that God's lives. We are the dwelling place of God. This is so because of the depth of love God has for us, His children.

Spend some time meditating on how important you are to God. Consider the depth of His love and compassion for you. Can you imagine starting to love and having compassion for yourself in the way God wills and purposes? Can you imagine how it would change your life and the way you live your life?

Let me tell you about a man named Tom. He was a hard worker and was very committed to providing for his family. When I met him, he was struggling with depression and anxiety. He expressed to me that his life was out of control, and if something did not change, he would lose everything that he had worked to accomplish.

Tom was well accomplished. He was making upwards of $600,000 per year, lived in a house worth $1.5 million, owned two BMWs, and had a healthy savings account.

I asked Tom how long it had been since he had taken some time for himself. He replied, "I have not taken a vacation in four years." He went on to say that when his family went on vacation he would stay behind to work, which was interesting because Tom could take time off work anytime. When asked about love and kindness towards himself, he replied, "I do not know what it means to love myself or to be loved." Tom thought that to love himself and to be loved by others was to simply work and provide for his family.

Have you ever felt even a tiny bit like Tom? That you do not deserve to be loved, or that the only way to receive love was to keep doing things for others? I encourage you to take some time and focus on God's love for you and how He wants you to embrace His love.

Self-compassion is critical in helping us deal with mental health challenges. Research has indicated that high levels of self-compassion can significantly abate the risk of depression and anxiety. It also improves optimism, increases focus and attention, and empowers you to recover faster from emotional challenges.

Principle Number Two: Love Others as Yourself.

There is a depth of truth in the proverbial saying: "you cannot give what you do not have." That is a profound truth worth pondering, especially when it comes to love.

There a song we sing at church that says, "give it with love." The point is that if you do not have love, you cannot give love.

Let us consider another profound question: What is love? Better yet, *who* is love?

In 1 John 4:7-21, the Bible tells us that "God is Love." Thus, for us to give love, we need to have God living in us. When He lives in us, we can express love, His love, to others.

There are two ways we can use loving-kindness meditation to demonstrate love and kindness to others. The first is love towards our family; the second is love towards our community.

Couples

When it comes to family, think of them in terms of units. First, meditate on what it means to love your wife or husband. The Bible tells us that we need to love them the same way Christ loves the church. It's true the Bible directs this command to the husband, but what if we apply it both ways? Take a moment to think about loving your wife or husband the way Christ loves the church.

Spend time to meditate and appreciate the attributes of your wife or husband. As you go about your daily activities, take a moment to bring your partner into focused attention. This practice will enhance resonance and strengthen attunement between you and your partner.

In the work of couples' guru Dr. John Gottman, he suggests numerous questions that couples can use to strengthen their relationship when thinking lovingly towards each other. Below is a list of Dr. Gottman 's questions.

- Meditate on one characteristic you find endearing or lovable about your partner.

- Meditate on one special (i.e. endearing, romantic, etc.) times in your relationship.

- Meditate on one physical attribute you love about your partner.

- Mediate on your partner's specific qualities. Affirm that you are proud to be married to them.

- Meditate on one thing that you both have in common. Affirm you have a genuine sense of "we" as opposed to "me" in this relationship.

- Meditate on one belief you share. Affirm how you have the same general beliefs and values.

- Meditate on a common goal you share together.

- Meditate on a time when your spouse was very supportive of you. Affirm that your spouse is very supportive.

- Meditate on one time that your spouse helped you reduce stress.

- Meditate on the first time you met your spouse.

- Meditate on one thing you both planned. Affirm how well you plan together and how you share a sense of control over your lives.

- Meditate on two things about your marriage that you are proud of. Affirm that you are proud of the relationship

- Meditate on one benefit of being in relationship with your partner. Affirm that you were fortunate to meet my partner.

- Meditate on one challenging thing that you have weathered together so far. Affirm that marriage is sometimes a struggle, but it is worth it.

- Meditate on doing or talking about something interesting. Affirm that you and your spouse are genuinely interested in one another.

- Meditate on a special trip you took together. Affirm that there is much healthy living in your relationship.

- Meditate about having made it through a hard time. Affirm that you can weather any storm together.

- Meditate on one good time in your relationship. Affirm that your relationship has had many good times.

Children and Parents

The second unit of family meditation has to do with parents or children demonstrating loving kindness towards each other. Loving-kindness meditation (parents towards children or children towards parents) entails meditative thoughts similar to the ones I stated in the previous section. I strongly recommend loving-kindness meditation towards each other daily.

Meditate on one characteristic you find endearing or lovable about your children or parents.

Meditate on a special time with your child or parents.

Meditate on one characteristic that makes you proud of your parent or child. Affirm that your parents or children have specific qualities that make you proud.

Meditate on one thing you have in common. Affirm that you feel a genuine sense of "we" as opposed to "me" in the relationship with my parent or children."

Meditate on one belief you share. Affirm you have the same general beliefs and values with your child or parent.

Meditate on a common goal you have with your child or parent.

Meditate on a time when your child/parents were very supportive of you. Affirm that they are supportive of you.

Meditate on one time when your parents/children helped you reduce stress.

Meditate on two things about your relationship with your parents/child that you are proud of.

Meditate on one challenging thing that you have weathered together so far as a family. Affirm that while relationships are sometimes a struggle, they are worth it.

Meditate on something to do or talk about that will engage your child or parents. Affirm that you are genuinely interested in each other.

Communities

Another critical component of biblical loving-kindness meditation is our openness to extending love and compassion to our communities. Jesus' command to his disciple and us is to deliberately reach out to our neighbors.

We live in a world that sometimes is void of love and compassion. We are called by Jesus to reach our communities with love, restore our communities with love, and reproduce love in our communities. I suggest that you start by visualizing your communities in positive, uplifting ways. This will enable you to feel gratitude for your community and arouse a sensation of love within you so you can extend love to your neighbors.

Biblical L

Loving-kindness meditation is a meditation of care, gentleness, tenderness, concern, friendship, and loving-kindness towards our communities. The practice of biblical loving-kindness meditation opens our mind and heart. It causes a desire for a deeper and more profound level of love in our hearts.

This type of meditation is void of any desire to possess one another. It is unconditional love, void of selfishness. It is a sentimental feeling of benevolence or obligation. Moreover, biblical loving-kindness meditation does not depend on relationships or how the other person feels about us; however, it requires a willingness to break down barriers between ourselves and others.

Let us look at a biblical narrative to demonstrate Loving-Kindness Meditation to others in our communities. I love the verse below in which Jesus takes time to love and care for a woman who has been rejected by society. It is found in John 4:

"Nevertheless, He needed to go through Samaria. So, He came to a city of Samaria called Sychar, near the plot of ground that Jacob gave to his son Joseph. Now Jacob's well was there. Jesus, therefore, being wearied from *His* journey, sat thus by the well. It was about the sixth hour. A woman of Samaria came to draw water.

Jesus said to her, "Give Me a drink," for His disciples had gone away into the city to buy food.

Then the woman of Samaria said to Him, "How is it that You, being a Jew, ask a drink from me, a Samaritan woman?" for Jews had no dealings with Samaritans.

Jesus answered, "If you knew the gift of God and who it is who says to you, 'Give Me a drink,' you would have asked Him, and He would have given you living water."

The woman said to Him, "Sir, you have nothing to draw with, and the well is deep. Where then do You get that living water? Are You greater than our father Jacob, who gave us the well and drank from it himself, as well as his sons and livestock?"

Jesus answered, "Whoever drinks of this water will thirst again, but whoever drinks of the water that I shall give him will never thirst. However, the water that I shall give him will become in him a fountain of water springing up into everlasting life."

The woman said to Him, "Sir, give me this water, that I may not thirst, nor come here to draw."

Jesus said to her," Go, call your husband, and come here."

The woman answered and said, "I have no husband."

Jesus said to her," You have well said, 'I have no husband,' for you have had five husbands, and the one you now have is not your husband; in that, you spoke truly."

The woman said to Him, "Sir, I perceive that You are a prophet. Our fathers worshiped on this mountain, and you *Jews* say that in Jerusalem is the place where one ought to worship."

Jesus said to her, "Woman, believe Me, the hour is coming when you will neither on this mountain nor in Jerusalem, worship the Father. You worship what you do not know; we know what we worship, for salvation is of the Jews. But the hour is coming, and now is, when the true worshipers will worship the Father in Spirit and truth, for the Father is seeking such to worship Him. God *is* Spirit, and those who worship Him must worship in Spirit and truth."

The woman said to Him, "I know that Messiah is coming (who is called Christ), when He comes, He will tell us all things."

Jesus said to her," I who speak to you am *He.*"

Notice verse four says, "But He needed to go through Samaria." Jesus was going from Judea to Galilee. This was a journey that Jews made frequently, but no Jew would go through Samaria because Samaritans were considered inferior. Again, look at Jesus' words, "He needed." Jesus *needed* to go through Samaria because He was consciously meditating through the Holy Spirit about a person who needed His help. This is a superlative example of Loving Kindness Meditation.

Loving-kindness meditation is selfless. It defies unhealthy societal norms and encourages us to consider the needs of others with deep love and compassion. Take some time and read the above narrative between Jesus and the woman and see how Jesus approaches her. Then, meditate on how you too might reach others in your community who are feeling rejected, abused, alone, marginalized, and/or oppressed.

As a young man growing up on the beautiful island of Jamaica, I often felt rejected and that I did not belong. I grew up with a loving father but got involved in dangerous things and lived a vile and ignoble life. People looked down on us and sometimes treated us like sub-humans.

But then someone reached out to me with the unconditional love of Jesus. The love and compassion they expressed changed my life. The moment I accepted the love and compassion of Jesus, my life did a complete turnaround.

Today I am where I am because someone shared loving kindness to me. This person told me that they spent time praying and meditating on how to reach me with the Love of Jesus. Praise God they reached out to me because if they had not, I would not be writing this book for you today.

Christo-centric Music Meditation: Rhythm

I would be remiss not to discuss music as a meditation method because music is a fundamental tool for healing and brain development. The heart of music is rhythm, and rhythm has the power to regulate the brain stem and integrate all aspects of cerebral operation. It literally harmonizes the diverse regions of the brain (known as "brain integration").

Rhythmical music in particular is one of the most effective methods of regulating and promoting brain integration. When Christ-centered music is included in the practice of biblical meditation, it promotes healthy growth in neural pathways and the myelination process of brain restoration.

I recommend choosing songs that focus on God, encourage understanding of His love and compassion, and invite you to reach out to Him through focused attention. This is what most worship groups refer to as 'praise and worship.' The Scripture says:

> "Speaking to yourselves in psalms and hymns
> and spiritual songs, singing and making melody
> in your heart to the Lord." (Ephesians 5:19)

From that scripture (and others), it is clear God endorses meditation through the use of music and Scripture together. Examples of Biblically recorded music are hymns, gospel music, and scripture songs.

In worship, I recommend starting with a short prayer. Here's an example to get you started:

"Lord, thank you for waking me this morning. Open my mind as I seek to worship you. Send your Holy Spirit to guide and teach me your ways and your desire for my life. Give me strength and wisdom from meditating on your Words. In your keep and care I commit my life, my struggles, and my ultimate victory. In Jesus' Name. Amen."

After you pray and your mind is in God's presence, worship with music. This might include singing, listening, or playing. I recommend two to three songs in every worship session. Hymns with lyrics such as, "Take my life and let it be consecrated Lord to Thee," and "All to Jesus I surrender, All to Him I freely give," or any other gospel song that speaks to your heart is appropriate. I will discuss the power of prayer in the next chapter.

Now let's take a moment to explore how music impacts different areas of the brain.

Christian music aids in the release of dopamine in the nucleus accumbens. Dopamine is responsible for experiencing pleasure and reward. Have you ever been to a place where you were listening to a song or musical piece and could feel joy running through your body like electricity? You were like experiencing the "rush" of dopamine.

Music plays an essential role in healthy attachment to God and others. When we listen to music, it draws us in and attaches us to its lyrical words and meanings, similar to how we grow attached to other things and people that bring us pleasure. Uplifting Christian music draws us closer to God and each other. It enables us to develop healthy dependent relationships with God and neighbor, which is due to the release of dopamine in the nucleus accumbens. The putamen is another brain structure closely related to the nucleus accumbens. Music also releases dopamine in this area of the brain.

These brain areas are responsible for processing rhythm and regulate body movement and coordination. Neuroscientist Kiminobu Sugaya says, "Music can increase dopamine and our response to rhythm." He goes on to say, "Music temporarily stops the symptoms of Parkinson's disease. Rhythmic music, for example, has been used to help Parkinson's patients' function, such as getting up and down and even walking because Parkinson's patients need assistance in moving. Music can help them, kind of like a cane. Unfortunately, after the music stops, the pathology comes back."

Hopefully you are starting to see how important music is to healthy brain function.

Music regulates the frontal lobe. The frontal lobe is important for thinking, decision making, and planning. Music enhances the functions of the frontal lobe, especially Christian music, which can help us function better at work, school, and daily living. For improved cognitive clarity, include music in your daily meditative practice.

Music also plays an important role in the temporal lobe. The temporal lobe processes what we hear and is the language center of the brain. Music integrates both sides of the brain. Often music has two components: words, and sounds. Words and language are interpreted in the left hemisphere of the temporal lobe, and music and sounds are interpreted in the right hemisphere of the temporal lobe. Thus, you can see how music functions to integrate both sides of the brain.

Two key language areas of the brain that are impacted by music are Broca's and Wernicke's areas. Broca's area is responsible for speech production. This is crucial for children in the language developmental stage. Music can help children express themselves more effectively; this is especially true of children who learn to play an instrument. Learning an instrument can help children become better communicators. Music activates the Wernicke area of the brain. This brain area is critical for comprehending written and spoken language. It is also used to analyze and enjoy music. Christian music aids in comprehending written and spoken language.

Given the impact of music on these two brain areas, it is essential for children and individuals with learning disabilities that affect language and comprehension to actively engage with music either by listening or playing an instrument.

The cerebellum is responsible for the storage of physical memory and coordinated movements. When we learn to play a musical instrument, the cerebellum improves memory retention, which can help individuals with Alzheimer's disease or those predisposed to Alzheimer's disease. It's no wonder that memories from early age musical instrument learning never fade away. Memories also play a significant role in helping individuals find purpose and happiness in the later stage of Alzheimer's disease.

Mindful Prayer

Meditative prayer involves uttering inner thoughts and yearnings to God. This complements the process of focused attention, which helps us receive intimate messages from God through scripture or inspiration. It also complements our response in loving-kindness meditation and helps us center our experience with God and reach out to humanity.

Moreover, meditative prayer enables us to be mindful of the present in worship and epitomizes the expression of our reciprocal interaction with God.

"Prayer is the opening of the heart to God as to a friend." (White, 2000).

The action of uttering either through whispering or audible conversation involves breathing and pacing one's self through spoken words.

Be aware that there is a difference between mindless prayer and mindful prayer. Mindless prayer excludes a reciprocal connection with God as described above. This is characterized by shallow breathing and impaired rhythmic movement of the breath. Mindful prayer ensures our minds are drawn to God as we connect with His work, mercies, and blessings.

Giving praise and thanksgiving, uttering in repentance, and active heart searching requires being present in the moment while engaging in what is called "paced utterance" to God. In the Jewish culture, this is known as chanting the sacred texts back to God. This process encompasses deep and rhythmic breathing.

When we practice prayer, our mind connects to God, but our brain structure starts to change with respect to the neuronal level. Prayer changes the brain by changing its neurons. As mentioned earlier, this process is called neuroplasticity.

The average human brain has approximately 100 billion neurons, and each neuron has at least 10,000 connections. That means there are over 1,000 trillion connections in the average human brain. Therefore, by praying, we can change the structure and function of our brain. Miraculously, each neuron in our brain is positively impacted when we communicate with God.

This fact is evidenced through the testimonies of countless individuals who profess that their lives, which were formerly filled with self-destructive behavior, were changed through the practice of humble, sincere prayer—even after trying everything else, including medication and psychotherapy.

Let us take a look at how Jesus teaches us to pray in Matthew 6:9-13:

"This, then, is how you should pray: "'Our Father in heaven, hallowed be your name, your kingdom come, your will be done, on earth as it is in heaven. Give us today our daily bread. And forgive us our debts, as we also have forgiven our debtors. And lead us not into temptation but deliver us from the evil one.'"

There are seven principles embedded in the Lords' prayer, all of which can RESTORE our minds.

Principle #1: REACH into the presence of God ("Our Father in heaven"). Jesus teaches us to reach or assent into the presence of God to have a personal encounter with God. Did you know that the moment you encounter God your brain begins to change? Yes, that is correct. The moment we move our mind into the presence of God our brain starts to change. Imagine getting a dose of neurological improvements on a constant basis. This is the reason Jesus implores us in Luke 18: " ...always pray and do not lose heart ..."

Principle #2: EMBRACE the holiness of God, ("holy be Your name"). In the presence of God there is holiness because we serve a holy and righteous God. Embracing God's holiness in His presence activates two key areas of the brain: the thalamus and the striatum.

The thalamus is the part of the brain that allows us to objectively see God to be real. It is the central sensory processing unit of the brain where all sensations, mood, and thoughts are sorted and distributed to other areas of the brain. The power of prayer to embrace God's holiness is the primary method God offers to help us objectively experience Him to be real. If we can see the realness of God in our lives it becomes easier for us to trust and be open to the things that He has in store for us.

The striatum, when activated by Mindfulness prayer, allows us to feel safe and secure in the presence of God. Sometimes we lose our sense of safety and security in the interior or exterior world. The reason Jesus teaches us to pray and acknowledge God is so we can experience a true sense of safety and security in His presence.

Principle #3: SUPPLICATE for heavenly principles to invigorate earth ("your kingdom come, your will be done, on earth as it is in heaven"). Research on prayer postulates that brief prayer, while it may be good for building healthy rituals, has not been proven to produce any direct effects on cognition. However, deep supplication, for the will of God to be done on a constant basis, enhances health and length of life.

Principle #4: TRUST that God will supply our needs ("give us today our daily bread"). Two other biblical words for *trust* are faith and belief. Humans have basic, innate needs. When our needs are not met, we tend to become stressed and weak. Hence Jesus implores us to ask and trust God to supply all our needs according to His riches.

Never forget this scripture. It is everything:

> "And my God will supply <u>all</u> my needs according to the riches of His glory in Jesus Christ." (Philippians 4:19)

We must ask God to supply our needs and believe that He will do it. It is important we do not doubt. The mental act of trusting God activates greater blood-oxygen level-dependent signals to all areas of the brain thus giving us strength and power and courage in our weakness moments.

Principle #5: OPENNESS to God's forgiveness ("And forgive us our debts"). Accepting God's forgiveness can be difficult for people. How can God forgive us for things we have done? Perhaps you have thought your sins are too "big" for God to forgive you?

Jesus said when we pray, we must be confident and open to the reality that God desires nothing more than to forgive and restore us so He can use us for His purposes.

Allow this to sink deep into your mind: there is nothing you can do that God has not already forgiven. To accept God's forgiveness is to embrace the reality that we serve a loving and compassionate God. Praying and meditating on acceptance of God's forgiveness is fundamental to adopting His divine character. The adoption of His holiness corresponds to our emotional connection to Him.

"Be holy because I am holy." (1 Peter 1:16)

Emotional regulation. Praying to a loving, compassionate, and forgiving God also activates the prefrontal cortex—more specifically, the anterior cingulate cortex. The anterior cingulate cortex helps regulate anger towards self and others, facilitates empathy and greater tolerance and acceptance of others, enhances emotional regulation, and improves the ability to be more loving towards self and others.

Notice in the Lord's Prayer how Jesus talks about acceptance of forgiveness before we can extend forgiveness to others. In other words, we need to experience God's amazing love and learn how to regulate our emotions before we can give it to others. As I said before, we can't give what we do not have.

Principle #6: REVEAL God's love to others by forgiving them ("as we also have forgiven our debtors"). In this life, we all experience painful events in which we are wounded, deceived, and betrayed by friends or family. These events may result in anger and hostility towards the person who caused us pain. We never want to minimize the pain, but Jesus appeals to us to seek forgiveness.

Did you know that the act of forgiving an offender is associated with positive emotional states? Think of it like this: you can reduce the emotional pain that the offender caused you by forgiving them.

Research indicates granting forgiveness is associated with improved brain function in the precuneus, right inferior parietal regions, and dorsolateral prefrontal cortex. These cerebral regions regulate theory of mind, empathy, and emotions. Clearly, God calls us to reveal His love to others by choosing to forgive them for their wrongs. Jesus said when you pray, pray mindfully for the desire to forgive others. He also said:

> "Blessed are the merciful for they shall be shown mercy." (Matt 5:7)

Principle #7: EQUIP us with power to defeat the attacks of the devil. ("And lead us not into temptation but deliver us from the evil one"). In this final principle, Jesus encourages us to mindfully pray for <u>power</u> to defend against the devil's attacks. The Bible says:

"For all that is in the world—the desires of the flesh and the desires of the eyes and pride of life—is not from the Father but is from the world." (1 John 2:16)

These three desires are the pivot upon which the devil builds his temptation scheme to dismantle the human family. There are three other words that are associated with the three schemes of the devil. They are impulses, desires, and urges. Think about it. Impulses, desires, and urges present the greatest challenges when we are faced with a decision. The antidote to managing desires, urges, and impulse is self-control. We must make a conscious effort to regulate our thoughts, actions, and emotions.

The area of the brain that empowers us to manage impulses, urges, and desires is the prefrontal cortex—more specifically, the dorsolateral prefrontal cortex. Mindfulness prayer activates the dorsolateral prefrontal. Hence, praying empowers us to resist temptation by activating the dorsolateral prefrontal cortex. The activation of the dorsolateral prefrontal cortex equips us to look at things objectively and make choices that are not based on urges, impulses, and unhealthy desires.

Now I hope that you have a different appreciation for the Lord's prayer. With this single prayer we have all the spiritual principles to R.E.S.T.O.R.E our minds. These principles are, R-reach, E-embrace, S-supplicate, T-trust, O-openness, R-reveal, and E-equip.

Conclusion

The principles discussed in this book are key elements in my ongoing transformation. I have shared with you techniques and practices that I used to facilitate the working of God in my life. It has been an amazing journey to reflect and see how God has been working in my life to transform my mind. These principles have helped to be a better man, father to my children, and husband to my wife. Like Paul says in Philippians 1:6 "And I am sure of this, that he who began a good work in you will bring it to completion at the day of Jesus Christ. God promised that He will complete the work that He started in my life and your life. Today I am no longer that angry, and vile thinking person I was at the beginning of my Journey with God. Why, I spend time daily, meditating on the work of God, listening to spiritual songs, memorizing bible verses and reaching out to others with love and compassionate.

To begin your journey today, there are ten things I want to recommend that you started doing right at this moment.

I.   Schedule three fifteen minutes section in your day for prayer and meditation.

II.   Source three uplifting spiritual songs per week that speak power into your life. Keep these songs in your mind constantly throughout your day.

III.   Search for 365 bible promises that declares peace, rest, joy, hope and love into your life. Memories and corelate one promise per day into your life.

IV.   Establish an intercessory prayer practice- Create a list of individuals that you are going to spend time each day interceding to God on behalf each one daily.

V.   Develop an attitude of gratitude-Being grateful and thankful promotes health of your body and mind. It empowers us against depression, anxiety, discontented thoughts and feelings

VI.   Smile daily- A joyful heart is good medicine, but a crushed spirit dries up the bones (Proverbs 17:22). Smiling has the power to regulate mood disorders and empower the brain to maintain a positive outlook on life. It enhances social interactions, empathy, and a sense of well-being.

VII. Seek to Cultivate positive imagination- ... whatever is honorable, whatever is just, whatever is pure, whatever is lovely, whatever is commendable, if there is any excellence, if there is anything worthy of praise, think about these things (Philippians 4:8). Trained your imagination to focus on elevated themes, themes, such as the ones mentioned in the above verse. These themes will empower your mind and enable you the empower the minds of others.

VIII. Extract the positive from the environment-Focusing on the negatives in the environment will only cover the mind in clouds of darkness. I invite to you redirect you mind to higher, loftier and nobler things. Talk of those things that will leave a good impression on the mind, and it will elevate you out of your circumstances into the light of hope.

IX. Redirect your mental energy-Allow your mind to focus on the rich provisions of the grace of God. God desires to change your life today, not tomorrow or in the future but today. He has provided everything for your transformation. Turn your eyes upon Jesus, because by beholding we become change (2 Corinthians 3:18).

X.   Identify someone to empower-We all know people in our lives who need an encouraging word. We can demonstrate love and compassion towards someone who may be experiencing a season of hopeless and despair. When our mind is filled with fear and worry, the mind cannot see the window of hope. Be that compass to direct someone today to the window of hope and it will electrify your mind.

If you desire to learn more about how to use biblical mediation to transform your life, connect with me today.

https://www.facebook.com/DrCourtneyDookie/?ref=bookmarks

www.drcourtneydookie.ca

drcourtneydookie@gnail.com

References

Brown, F., Driver, S., & Briggs, C. (2008). *The Brown-Drivers-Briggs Hebrews and English lexicon.* Massachusetts: Hendrickson publishers, Inc.

Dookie, Courtney (2017). Neuroplasticity: Healing the brain from psychological disorder through Biblical meditation.

White, Ellen G. (1977) Mind, Character, and Personality Volume 2. Nashville, TN: Southern Publishing Association.

Emiliano Ricciardi, Giuseppina Rota, Lorenzo Sani

Claudio Gentili, Ann Gaglianses, Mario Guazzelli and Pietro Pietrini. (2013). How the brain heals emotional wounds: the functional neuroanatomy of forgiveness. Frontiers in human neuroscience.

Knoch, Daria., Fegr, Ernst. (2007). Resisting the power of temptations, the right prefrontal cortex and self-control. Institute for Empirical Research in Economics, University of Zurich, Blumlisalpstrasse, Zurich, Switzerland

Lucina Q. Uddin, Nomi S. Jason, Hebert-Seropian Benjamin, Ghaziri, Jimmy, and Boucher, Olivier Structure and function of the human insula. (2017). J Clin Neurophysiology.

Newberg, Andrew, Waldman, Mark. (2009). How God changes your brain. Ballantine books trade: New York.

John 3:16

About the Author

Dr. Dookie is a Registered Provisional Clinical Psychologist. He is passionate about helping individuals find true transformation and renewing of their minds. He is the founder of Mind Renewal Ministry and currently serves as a clinical psychologist with his wife in their private practice Dookies' Psychological Services in Northern Alberta.

He has his Doctoral degree in Clinical Psychology, with an emphasis in developmental trauma. He achieved his BA in Theology at Northern Caribbean University, Jamaica and MA in Spiritual Care and Psychotherapy at Wilfrid Laurier University, Canada. Dr Dookie has been providing individuals and couples therapy since 2012. He specializes in developmental trauma and addiction therapy (substance use, gambling addiction, gaming addiction, pornography addiction), and mental health therapy (PTSD, depression, anxiety, eating disorder). Other supports he provides include self-esteem, stress management, anger management, holistic counselling (physical, emotional and spiritual).

Dr. Dookie is a speaker, mind expert, and mentor who does workshops and seminars on the following topics: How God designs the mind, parenting your child's mind, healing the mind and brain through biblical meditation, how prayer transforms the mind, God's plan to restore the mind, and the ten principles for mind growth. He is the author of two books, Neuroplasticity: Healing the Brain from Psychological Disorders through Biblical Meditation and Christian Contemplative Meditation Practice: How Biblical Contemplative Practice Facilitates Neuroplasticity in Adults who have Experienced Developmental Trauma.

Printed in the United States
By Bookmasters